Do Not Peel the Birches

For Bill,
Thanks for a wonderful evening.

Fleda Brown Jackson

Fleda Brown

Oct 2001

Do Not Peel

the Birches

PURDUE UNIVERSITY PRESS / WEST LAFAYETTE, INDIANA

Design by Chiquita Babb
Printed in the United States of America

LIBRARY OF CONGRESS CATALOGING-IN-PUBLICATION DATA

Jackson, Fleda Brown, 1944–
  Do not peel the birches / Fleda Brown Jackson.
    p.   cm.
  ISBN 1-55753-040-8 (alk. paper)
  I. Title.
PS3560.A21534D6   1993
811'.54—dc20   92-41176
                                                   CIP

This book is for Kelly and Scott

Grateful acknowledgment is given to the following magazines in which these poems have appeared, sometimes in different versions:

American Literary Review, "After the Rain," "Then You Fall in Love, at Your Age"

Ariel, "Bread," "Snow"

Beloit Poetry Journal, "The Location of Fleda Phillips Brown," "The Farthest-North Southern Town"

Brigham Young University Studies, "The Route We Take"

Croton Review, "A Few Miles from Homestead" (also reprinted in *Anthology of Magazine Verse and Yearbook of American Poetry*, 1988)

Georgia Review, "A Long and Happy Life" (also reprinted in *Anthology of Magazine Verse and Yearbook of American Poetry*, 1989)

Indiana Review, "Do Not Peel the Birches"

Iowa Review, "For Michelle," "Mississippi River, Near Cape Girardeau," "Learning to Dance," "Ballroom Dancing," "If I Were a Swan," "Flashlight Tag," "An Introduction"

Mid-American Review, "Cedar River," "Burdett Palmer's Foot" (winner of the James Wright Prize for poetry, vol. 11)

Midwest Quarterly, "Roanoke: The Lost Colony"

Pembroke, "Anhinga," "A Few Lines from Rehoboth Beach"

Southern Humanities Review, "Bombay Hook," "Olga Knipper to Anton Chekhov, January 1902"

Stone Country, "Dock"

Sycamore Review, "Minnow"

West Branch, "Dunes," "Night Swimming"

Yarrow, "Four Poems for Kelly," "St. Pete Beach"

I wish to express my gratitude to the University of Delaware for a summer grant which supported me in my work on some of these poems, and to Jeanne Walker, Jerry Beasley, and Elaine Terranova for their friendship, support, and suggestions. I am also grateful to Gerald Stern for his help with final revisions.

CONTENTS

I

II

III

IV

It could not be dangerous to be living
        in a town like this, of simple people,
who have a steeple-jack placing danger signs by the church
while he is gilding the solid-
        pointed star, which on a steeple
stands for hope.

                            —Marianne Moore
                            "The Steeple-Jack"

I

DO NOT PEEL THE BIRCHES

In his time,
germs were found to be everywhere,
especially in his ball-and-socket joint
which was welded together by tuberculosis germs
before pasteurized milk became a rule.
Grandfather ordered his shirts done at home
because (he demonstrated) the downtown launderer
spat germs on the iron to test the heat.
Flies (he caught mid-flight in his cupped hand)
could crop-dust germs over lunch,
and one's mouth grew germs quickly enough
between the meal and the toothbrush.

He gathered us at Central Lake every summer
to learn the rules. He explained the use of
lie (to recline) and *lay* (to place or put):
because of his lame leg, he could *lie*
comfortably only in the canoe, so we must
lay it gently on the sand, keeping its
irreplaceable wooden frame from rocks.

At Central Lake, one could get hold
of things that go wrong. One could nail a sign
on the birches to save their delicate skins.
One could avoid shampoos or detergents that foam
the lake. One could rinse diapers in a bucket
far up the hill to filter the dirty water
through the ground. One could wait
one full hour after meals, and only swim
across the lake guarded by the rowboat.
One could follow the rules and get results.

When Grandfather was ninety-four
he was still getting results.
In the cottage, he heard the wind chimes
answer to an ancient wind.
Someone pulled diapason
on the pump organ, and he called back
a perfectly metered hymn.
Muttering through the fir trees, he
was able at last to discuss the day's mail
with his dead wife, who knew what to do.
And every morning and evening,
he stoppered his ears, hitched his lame leg
over the dock, and buried himself in the lake,
only his nose rising for air. He broke through
the elements as cleanly as a machine.

MINNOW

It is not the way it used to be.
Aunt Cleone is losing her memory,
my father refuses to paint the cottage porch,

the rowboat rots in the yard. I am
willing to let go of what I remember,
not completely, but let it open out

into the past and fill it and funnel
forward to this place where I actually
lie on the end of the dock swirling my finger

in the water, watching the minnows
move without seeming to move, invisible
twitches, one, two, three minnows the color

of sand. I must be in the middle
of my life, the way I feel balanced
between one thing and another. As if I have

no hands or arms, parting the world
as it reaches my face. Like a minnow, gone
on little wings, a blush of sand from the bottom.

Sometimes I open my eyes in the dark
and it feels as if I'm moving. I lose
my loneliness, surrounded with dark, like water.

LEARNING TO DANCE

When we waltzed with the senior citizens
at the Pappy Burnett Pavilion,
I felt how you moved slick as a cowboy,
my own rough bones clicking beside
you, trying to move the way trying can't
go. I loved you, turning in yourself
like a loose skin, and the woman
who danced with her broom, and the old man
round-dancing, his shirt open over
his heavy belly, an old, old grace
feeding him from the bass
of the country band. I've always
wanted to dance. Aspen leaves tambourine
in the wind, needles flare from the tamarack
branch like ballet skirts, and that
Wednesday of the Central Lake Pavilion Dance
travels miles in place, turning
and returning to its original dark.
Afterward, I pulled off my swimsuit in the lake
and held you next to me, learning
from your heart and the slap slap of waves
on stones. What is it wants us to know
where to step? Each pause
brings us tight against the mouth
of the earth, and then we raise one
foot like the flame of a candle.
Our bodies move in and out of the space
we've held to be true, and something else
sees each half turn as the whole dance.

THE ROUTE WE TAKE

1

The lake is a droop of space
and we are paddling in it,
remote and yearning.
An old man and woman start out
in their pontoon boat that sputters
weeds. We find them again,
farther on, fishing. The woman
has balanced her hips on a twig
of a chair. The man spits
at the water as if he has arrived
at exactly the right place.

2

A root floats up,
a gladiator's arm,
brown-studded, crooked.
Cut, it feels like cork,
or something you could
eat if you had to,
one thing standing for
another, and nothing
as horrible as it looks,
snaked underwater.

3

Two great blue heron jut
fantastically, pterodactyl-
beaked, carrying the sky
to a cold distance. The high
sun sinks its teeth
in the waves. We arch
our necks after the bird.
The last thing we want,
we tell ourselves, is
intelligence, or comfort.

4

Dick says they subpoenaed
the farmer who penned hogs
across a feeder-stream,
their raw fecal matter
launching out, greening.
We stop and wade to where
the cold appears invisible.
We actually drink from our
hands, praying for innocence.

5

We follow the mink along
the bank until it climbs
into the tangle of roots
where water has risen
and fallen. We see through
to clearings, stammers
of light, a few sharp red
cardinal flowers, a whole
network of traces, not ours.

6

A row of old docks slope
and dislodge like disproved
theories. We observe
the sequence
of them, heavy and frail.
Lily pads collect
at their feet to soften
the failure. The day
is full of sunshine. We have
our canoe, our traveling.

7

Late evening, we pass
through the needle's eye
of the bridge. Our big
voices briefly catch
between the concrete roof
and black water, before
we open into our own
wide lake, our faces
extinguishing, no one to tell
if the paddle is feathered,
no crucial place.

FLASHLIGHT TAG

I am the one with the flashlight,
in a sweat, trusting my feet
through the trees. This was
my sister's idea, gathering us all
to play flashlight tag
like when we were kids.
Now we are grown up, with
our own kids, and still, everyone's
hiding in the soft leaves.
My tooth of light casts sudden
black trunks, breaks open
the grass, jolts rocks along the shore.
I remember myself curled
between two trees, the Indian feet
of the big boys anywhere at all,
the whole world moving in
against my small self, turned nose
down to the clicks and shuffles
of the night. There used to be
a loon in Osborne's pond,
its cold yodel floating across
the road to where I lay. I am still
curled inside the soft nest
of myself, even while I aim
the radical light. . . . I flush out
my sister Linnie first,
and she takes my hand like a child,
and we feed each other the old
fears, half laughing, running.
Then we wait, bound the way
we've always been, not wanting

to stir up the night. Let
the others fall asleep, or come on
back to the fire by themselves.
It has taken us years to hold hands
again, to remember how plainly
the darkness sees us, always
as if we were eight years old,
the battle of our parents rising
and crashing through the night,
and we far under the covers,
turned breath to breath, one breath.

THE LOCATION OF
FLEDA PHILLIPS BROWN

I think my grandmother stays mostly
in this part of the lake, maybe
up to Birch Point,
down to Deepwater Point,
her ashes churning behind big boats,
rocking against the shore, ashes
in the perches' mouths,
ashes in the ribbon of sun
under the water, ashes raining
through the hemlocks.
I swam in her for years, not knowing.
Before I found out, I had one
definite story, me, on my knees
on her iron bed, running the ivory
brush down her hair while she
found the book's good distance
from her eyes, went on,
in her school-voice:

                            "Rather than
study grammar," said Gigino,
"I would change myself into an ant,
one of those ants that go about
always on parade, and do nothing
but march from morning to night."
So heaven turned Gigino into
White Patch the Ant, who carried
his little spot of earth
like a briefcase, learned
what it means to work.

Waves of loosened braid,
yellow and iron down her back,
that close I came to touching her!
For thirty-five years,
after the funeral in East Chatham,
or Troy, where I heard they had
folding chairs and Beethoven's Ninth
on the phonograph, she
brushed against me on all sides,
a fine grain. All that
about work: she could have just
opened my pores and passed through,
and did, and nobody told me anything.

LOON CRIES

Unless there is a loon cry in a book, the poetry has gone out of it.
—*Carl Sandburg*

Three loons appear in this poem, two
on one side of the canoe, one
on the other, but

not stable. One drops down
to nothing, emerges two minutes later
twenty feet away, quavering

his black beak's cold cries
across us to the others like a natural
bridge: oo-AH-hoo. Three loon cries

arise in this poem
from a hollow carved out
of itself, the slosh of what it says

to itself, not to us.
We four in the canoe sit
in the open AH, riding low as loons.

No one knows who feels
what, or how much. The grieving
syllables lie over us, untouchable

oo-AH-hoo, yodeled
oo-AH-hoo. Oh Lord, if we knew
what we can take from each other, and what

we have to leave alone,
if we knew which maniacal dives
the universe was thinking of all along.

NIGHT SWIMMING

We are without our men, hers dead
ten years, mine far away, the water
glassy warm. My old aunt already stands
half in. All I see is the white half,
her small old breasts like bells,
almost nice as a girl's. Then we hardly
feel the water, a drag on the nipples,
a brush on the crotch, like making love
blind, only the knives of light
from the opposite shore, the shudders
of our swimming breaking it up.
We let the water get next to us
and into the quick of losses we don't
have to talk about. We swim out
to where the dock goes blank,
and we are stranded, abandoned good flesh
in a black of glimmering. We each fit
our skin exactly. After a while
we come out of the water slick as eels,
still swimming, straight-backed,
breasts out, up to the porch,
illuminate, sexy as hell, inspired.

AUNT CLEONE WORKS HARD
AT RECYCLING

After dark, Aunt Cleone happens across
the trash bags stacked, and begins to go through them,
finding strips of perfectly good
cloth to wash, cans to flatten, bottles to soak
the labels off. She is sad for our waste,
and she gathers armloads to her room,
stacks flattened cardboard under her bed,
lines up bottles on her shelves.
All these! Where's the next breath
coming from? Her mother's and father's voices,
beloved and quite saved, grow smaller,
the way the two of them turned to dots, swimming off
in the morning sun toward Snowflake.
But then back again.
Her mother's black wool swimming suit
still hangs on its nail like a bat.

In the morning, she has forgotten
the trash. I find it in piles on the kitchen floor,
what she forgot when she fell asleep, sorting.
She sits on the porch, stitching
someone's old blouse to fit her.
"Look," she says, "at the sunlight
reflecting like fire on the white sides
of the sailboat. It burns, but it never burns
anything up."
That's what I see, looking up.
Looking down, I see tiny suns dashing
like stray curls off the bottom of the water.
I notice we've kept the same sun and moon
we've always had, among all the suns and moons.

Today particularly, my father seals up
his camera in a tupperware bowl
with silica gel to keep it dry.
He wraps large rubber bands cut from
an old inner tube around the bowl.
Aunt Cleone is fixing a bowl of raw oatmeal,
yogurt, and sesame seeds.
She takes a damp undershirt from the refrigerator
and unwraps enough purslane and mint leaves
to grind on her cereal. They are arguing
about sex. My father says women don't like it.
Cleone tells how she and Uncle Bob
made love every day after swimming, how she
wore him out. My mother takes her toast
to the patio and watches a huge jay land
spread-legged on the rail,
scattering goldfinches away from the feeder.
This is as close to the facts
as I can get. It is Thursday, 9:20,
after a cold swim. Cleone enters her twenty-third
year without a cold or any other sickness.
My mother has almost succeeded at solitude.
Even the jay is no sorrow to her.

MY FATHER TAKES
MY RETARDED BROTHER SAILING

They tack up and down
all morning, Mark trailing one hand

in the waves, crying his hard
gull-cries of joy, my father pointing out

bright flags on shore, which are
us, waving

them on, until
the sudden commotion of sail, jabber

of cleats, swingabout of
boat, pivot of Central Lake on

my father's foot, caught at that moment
in a rope,

my father hanging neither up
nor down, thrashing under, using,
                    maybe using up his lungs

to catch that child who hardly knows
water from air. The thought,

oh yes, the thought settles
in my heart: part of me

goes down, drowned, the perfect part
splashes back

to shore. And then years
later, here I come,

bringing out the towels, willing
as a murderer, reformed, but sentenced

anyway, to this life, to this
abundant life in which they have both

come back, my father's ankle bloody
from the rope, my purple-lipped

brother riding his shoulders,
                    uncontrollably babbling.

SUNDAY AT THE LAKE

We all arrive at the Congregational Church
where on this particular Sunday the "Messengers
of Melody" from Muskegon are singing
the sermon. Irvin, his vest wearing his name,
squeezes out "Jerusalem" as if he knows something
urgent we should do. Then the whole group sings
"Marching in the Blood-Washed Band," and then
the youngest boy tells how the kids on his bus
all play their rock 'n' roll, but he has to
let them know he likes God's music best. After
this we shake hands, and outside I pick
some malva along the curb for Aunt Cleone,
and we coast to the restaurant, my father
swearing dammit he's not going to use
gas downhill. We all order the chicken dinner special
except Aunt Cleone, who spreads out her wilting
malva on her purse in her lap, and eats it
a sprig at a time. She asks her share of the bill,
but we tell her the water is free. After that
we go home to the cottage, where my father gets out
his screwdriver and tries to adjust his Westclox,
which has lost three minutes overnight.

While we are having breakfast
on the screened-in porch, waffles
with blueberries, my mother wrinkles
into tears over nothing, some
remembrance. She is always
giving in. The outside world is
wrung out, too, exhausted
with last night's rain, darkened
and earthly. On the black tree trunk,
a nuthatch pitches itself
upside down and sideways,
pecking wildly for bugs
under the bark. A chickadee
is a quick breath, lifting
off a limb. I want
to take my mother's hands,
but they are almost transparent,
terrible on the table.
Her body hunkers like a vase,
accumulating sorrows. It is
a Chinese vase, slender
at the neck, glazed
on the inside. In my mouth
are scrambled eggs
I have to eat or never get up
again. I sit through adolescence,
adulthood, safely
into menopause. The eggs soften
in my mouth, harden on
my plate, yellow ruffles.
Blue flowered oilcloth clings

to the table. My mother's hands
keep on fluttering
outward. No use, no use.
I pass her a waffle, butter,
the jug of pure
maple syrup, too heavy to pour.
I line up these items
in front of her. Hope
tries to get out of my chest.
It sounds like my heart, but it's
furious, hungry, light as a bird.

CEDAR RIVER

The earth is laid down dead
and alive at once, soft
and leaking from every vein
into the utterly clear creek.
Under the cedars a dead deer's bones
gather against the shade, the teeth
in the jawbone still firm
and musical, surer than my feet
through here. A porcupine big
as a small bear climbs unafraid
among the logs. Her quills
are streaks of sunlight and shade.
She walks back into the woods
with a sleepy ease
like a pregnant woman. I try
to follow across the weave
of roots, but it is like being
underwater. She crawls
over a mound of washed-up
twigs, one heap of twigs
becoming the other, like a Picasso
painting, and all over
the trees, eyes watching
from their separate
branches, separate planes.
I try to sort them out, using
logarithms, exponents,
the damndest of metaphors.
One Grass-of-Parnassus flower
stands at the edge of the bracken,

almost in the water, five white
petals with five purple
veins, hard little rivers headed
straight for the center of the world.

THE SONS OF THE PROPHET
ARE BRAVE MEN AND BOLD

He used to climb that tall pine
on the edge of Osborne's land
(but, as his parents ordered, still
on his own land) and sing
"Abdul Abulbul Amir" at the top
of his lungs, all verses.
I can imagine that—his playing
the notes out in his level
folksinger's voice, as if he had
to keep them on the branch,
finally hearing the story inside
himself, the whole war of it,
until he climbed into it and escaped
to the heart, where Ivan kills Abdul
and Abdul kills Ivan, the sons
of the prophet lie sprawled,
and only the wind threads the pine
tops. I know all that
as he sings the song again tonight
in his deliberate old voice,
how it lifted him, how it carried him
many times on a sword blade
over the property line, his father
far below, green visor keeping
the sun off his book. The legs
of his father's chair punch squares
in the slope where the
legendary anthill has just begun.
Already, the ants are carrying
their underground loads step by step
toward the surface.

This is thirty years before
he himself scattered boric acid
over the huge mound, no harm
to the soil, but killing the ants
by the futile scrapings of their own
legs, little violin bows, wearing
the crystals through their chitin.

HOW MY FATHER GOT RELIGION

He got, with his grandmother's gifts
of Bible books or handkerchiefs
on alternating Christmases,
her admonitions and prayers.
To counteract this, his father held
two rocks behind his back.
He hit them together. "Can you hear these?"
he asked. "Can you hear God?"
Then he held them in front. "Can you see
these?" he asked. "Can you see God?"
Every afternoon at the lake
my father had to lie in the hammock
and read Herbert Spencer for two hours,
to learn how God got accidentally
cupped in the lips, one fantastic
syllable for the scattered sky
and earth. Even then, he would drift off.
He had an eye for the boats,
the way they find and take the wind.
In seventy years he learned how
to build them nearly perfectly.
"Can you see that?" he asks me, pointing
down the line of the hull.
"As little resistance as a wooden boat
can make," he says. We wade out,
with our lifejackets. Up goes the great
white handkerchief, down
the centerboard bolts. Nothing
moves, then a catch
of wind, the sloop-sloop beginning,
amplified in the hollow of the deck.

The shore picks up speed.
He reads the wind shadow off the point,
the advancing gust scraping its feet
on the whitecaps. "Say it's three miles
to town," he says. He checks his watch,
begins to figure knots.

IF I WERE A SWAN

I would ride high
above my own white
weight. I would ride
through the lightening
of the earth
and the darkening,
stillness and turbulence
coming on in the core
of me, and spreading
to the hard rain,
to the dazzle. Leaves
would turn, but I
would keep my eyes
in my head, watching
for grasses. This
is what I would know
deeply: the feathering
of my bones
against the bank.
For the rest,
I would be the easiest
wave, loving just enough
for nature's sake.
The world would move
under me and I would
always be exactly
where I am, dragonflies
angling around my head.
Under the black mask
of my face, I would think
swan, swan,

which would be nothing
but a riding, a hunger,
a ruffle more pointed
than wind and waves,
and a hot-orange
beak like an arrow.

LETTER HOME

Grass River is a snake on the tongue.
You, love, a thousand miles down
the map, many turns. Meanwhile,
I am plunging ahead here through
forget-me-nots, marsh marigolds,
Joe Pye weed, and underneath,
the bright fur of mosses,
moss over moss, tangled, unspoken,
this great green marsh bleeding
everywhere.

        Speckled trout line up
like knives under the falls; strings
of moss weave and pull, one
hard pull, everything part-
ing, everything in slits, peaks
of reflected light, teeth, laughter.
If you were here, it would be
just the same, only two,
taking on whole the foreign language
of the birds. It would cling
to nothing in us, and we would still
be hungry together, teeth, tongues.

STONES

Cousin Al remembers the old game
he's still good at. You take
a stone from shore, large enough
to pull you to the bottom, but not
so big you can't bring it back
to hold the bank in place.
You swim out until the bottom
is as far below as you can bear.
Al shows me how to clear
my ears as I drop, but as soon
as they feel the squeeze, I see
how hard the stone pulls
down, how slow my rise will be.
My mother will finally leave
my father holding the refrigerator
door open, still explaining
geography. Aunt Cleone will forget
even yogurt, fade into silvery
fur between the birch trees.
My daughter will finish
graduate school, my son become
a computer programmer. The sun
will rise and set on opposite sides
of where I was last seen. This
is one second before my hands
let go the rock. I am a woman
on the way up: lungs, stomach,
heart, uterus, all my precious
cavities holding their own.
No doubt Al's won again, already

pushed off from below. Me, I'm
composed of space and the fear
of space. They break
the surface arguing like lovers.

DOCK

Say *dock, dock:* it's just a hollow
of itself, the way the foot
echoes between wood and water,
the plank, plank of it
like piano keys, growing hollower
farther out under the stars.
Listen to the way *dock's* closed in
by the tongue on one side, pushed out
at the far end toward the lake
with a duck-sound, quack-
sound, where they congregate
for crumbs. It's even a tongue,
itself, saying nothing but
what you bump against it.
Or an arm, reaching out. Here
you're willing to make yourself sociable,
declare yourself separate
from the trees. "Dock here,"
you offer. Here is a place
to stop. And it's true. Indeed,
I have to stop at the end,
and think. The reason
for walking out here is
how the end goes blunt.
You feel your blood turn back
toward the heart, but
for an instant, you imagine,
it longs to keep moving out,
like Roadrunner at the edge of a cliff,

keeping on with nothing built
to hold him up. Turning back,
I carve a cul-de-sac in the air,
which is a comfort, and a sadness.

II

BURDETT PALMER'S FOOT

You spend the night trying to dodge
patches of wet soybean meal that smell
like shit. One of the things you smell, though,
that wonderful wood, coming out of Natchez,
going north. But there's the soybeans,
the boxcars full of fishmeal, and chemical
cars, leaking gasses. I'd work all night
with the lantern, checking cars and contents,
then the light would start coming up
behind the shapes of flatcars, wood cars,
boxcars, tankers. About five, I'd stop
at the beanery under the railroad bridge
for chili so bad after a while it was good.
The morning I saw the foot, two boxcars
stood misplaced in front of the beanery,
a crowd around the shoe, beside the rails.
They said Burdett stepped between the couplings
just as the links pulled tight and sliced
the bottom off his foot. Everything stayed
put, waiting for inspectors out of Chicago.
I was only seventeen, so I had to stick
my nose in the shoe, to see the private insides
of a foot. Burdett Palmer's foot, that
stayed too long in the same place. I needed
to see it close, and then I needed the long
sight north, a mile down track where the light
came to a point. Overhead, the huge arched
bridge left the boxcars and beanery as long
as it possibly could, before coming down.

Dear friend you were right: the smell of fish and foam
and algae makes one green smell together. It clears
my head. It empties me enough to fit down in my own

skin for a while, singleminded as a surfer. The first
day here, there was nobody, from one distance
to the other. Rain rose from the waves like steam,

dark lifted off the dark. All I could think of
were hymns, all I knew the words to: the oldest
motions tuning up in me. There was a horseshoe crab

shell, a translucent egg sack, a log of a tired jetty,
and another, and another. I walked miles, holding
my suffering deeply and courteously, as if I were holding

a package for somebody else who would come back
like sunlight. In the morning, the boardwalk opened
wide and white with sun, gulls on one leg in the slicks.

Cold waves, cold air, and people out in heavy coats,
arm in arm along the sheen of waves. A single boy
in shorts rode his skimboard out thigh-high, making

intricate moves across the March ice-water. I thought
he must be painfully cold, but, I hear you say, he had
all the world emptied, to practice his smooth stand.

MISSISSIPPI RIVER,
NEAR CAPE GIRARDEAU, MO.

My father and I take our usual walk
by Cape Girardeau's sea wall that steers
the river as fast as possible past us,
from Minneapolis to the sea. The wall's
spray-painted with messages of love and hate
along the river side. And with eagles.
Some skill went into them. One perches,
a Harley Davidson logo, brand name below
the sketch, the other bird in full flight,
and under it, Isaiah: "They shall mount up
with wings as eagles." Some Huck Finn, here,
still shakes off the weight of widows
and deacons—Oh motorcycles, wings, rushing
water! I have not had freedom in my life.
Crossing these granite rocks on shore,
I think, now, at this age, how it would be
to kill the wild pig and light out in a canoe.
Those on shore could bury my memory.
It would do no good for my father to weep.
The long river would dash me to the gulf,
where the land would open its hips
and I would float into clarity, and a sweet
brine. The water under me would turn to sky.
My canoe would be a smile, and I would
paddle from island to island, saving lives.

ST. PETE BEACH

I am drinking coffee alone
in the Country Village Restaurant
in St. Pete Beach while the man
I love is still asleep in the bare
efficiency we've taken for two days.
It's one very small bed, one roach
trap beside the bed, one table, one
stove, in a small resort sandwiched
between the bay and gulf. Away
from home, we become delicately poised
on the globe. Night after night, we
arrive at motels after dark, and I
wake up in some place I've never
seen. My old ways hardly matter.
I have to take care of myself, and
love myself, and be as perfectly
whole as I can, not knowing what
world I am in, only the bed, chair,
sink, table, one of everything. I
start loving each word I speak to the
waitress at breakfast, thinking if I
phrase the question right, she might
tell me something that will help.

A FEW MILES FROM HOMESTEAD

It is off-season, and the Mikasuki Indian
in a red T-shirt that reads
JOSIE BILLY FOR TRIBAL CHIEF
has only us on his airboat, he
on the throne before the huge propeller,
we on our choice of seats with our childhood
fantasy of skimming above the fringe
of swamp in the roar of a Cadillac engine.
At the end of his casual route,
he has set up a village of two thatched huts
where his wife and mother sit
at their sewing machines, piecing together
bright cloth, neither looking up from a gloom
that seems like some great knowledge.
Standing beside the jar marked "Tips,"
the son shows us his baby alligators.
He is an old hand at the smile,
the discussion of lizards and coots.
We drop too much money in the jar,
which makes the family speak Hichiti
softly among themselves. We are
more strangers than ever, exact and fretful.
This is reservation land, where our laws
are eased like a deep sigh across
the grasses, but we arrive as our forefathers
did, to set foot on any shores we come to,
to take what we can find, to lift
it away from its great silence, which
we break and break, as soon as we're
returned to the dock. For miles
down Route 41, we talk about our mothers,

our fathers, the loss of their love
as if it had been perfectly stored on some
shelf in the earliest house we remember,
and we had failed to look hard enough.

ANHINGA

The anhinga is spread on the bush
like a rag, drying its watersoaked
wings. It must have just gone under
for a fish, and now it takes
a long time in the sun, snaking
its neck to smooth and pick its oil-
less feathers, one by one. We get tired
of waiting to see it fly. In all
that time, a purple gallinule steps
from lilypad to lilypad, four turtles
drift underwater. Behind the anhinga lies
pa-hay-okee, the river of grass.
Haven't you ever longed for preparations
to end? Did the anhinga ever actually
break the water? Sometimes even
the real world is a park where nothing
happens, but you think about what
once happened, or what might
happen. You walk the paths, barely
able to contain your wish.
The animals turn away into their
peculiar shapes. This is what makes you
start telling lies, waving your hands
to illustrate, wagging your finger,
as you leave the anhinga for dead
with its hundreds of feathers.

ST. PAUL'S AND ST. GEORGE'S CHURCH, EDINBURGH

I choose this shell of a church because I want to see
what God does when He lasts more years than people

can afford. It's an ordinary parish church, but large,
its tympanums and gargoyles drying out, holding on.

It is Sunday morning. On one side of me, a man sits down
turning his gap-teeth my way, wafting his body

like a thurible of cheap wine and bitter old human smell.
A woman slides in on the aisle side, pinning me in,

almost touching me, her face all one scar, vacant
from this angle as a half-moon! Her eyes sink

to asymmetrical wells, her hair floats in patches.
Under her warped mouth, another mouth, a smiling scar.

She sits against me in this vast space, a horrible
accident who probably can't afford repairs.

It starts up. The old man knows all the words and says
them every one off-rhythm. A hull tender to the quick,

the face of the woman knows how to be exactly itself.
What am I? A child. Nothing but a child,

caught by my own grace, my own new smell. And here comes
God, creaking down the nave, level-eyed.

MOTHER-OF-THE-BRIDE DRESS

I'm walking around the outer roped-off
circle of Stonehenge considering whether
the dress I've ordered for your wedding is
after all exactly what you want me to wear:
it's aqua, several shades lighter than
the teal blue you said, with beads on bodice
and sleeves. If I were a pre-Druid woman,
entering this dread eclipse between the hinge-
stones, the color of my dress would hide me
in the sky. I would be beady sky, leading
you. You would look like swallowed light,
and all around us the silence would be filled
with distance, and sheep. My shoes, dyed
to match my dress, would punch holes of sky
in the grass. In these ancient rituals, all
existence wants to face the sun! The way
not to disappear, dear one, is to start talking.
Once we entered the inner horseshoe of stones,
I would tell you everything about the past. By
the time the final blows of sun landed
on the bluestones, I would have you caught up,
at last. We would look at each other
in elaborate detail, laugh like temple bells.

My hairdresser Frank's own hair's cut punk
today, livid as a ruffled bird.
He tells me about his brother-in-law
on the police force who tells him how
the cops punch out the punks on Main Street,
and get away with it, too. They got
these leather gloves, he says, with brass
inside, so no bruises show, and even
if there are some, they're gone
by the time the trial comes up, or the judge
will say you might have fallen down
stairs. This town is the farthest-north
Southern town, Frank says, switching scissors,
and nobody wants to argue with the mayor,
who appoints the police chief, and so on,
like a ricochet bullet, down
to your basic level of cop who takes
his shift to count the number of times
the same car cruises Main Street
in an hour. Three time's the limit.
Then out he comes, his cruiser flashing
red and blue. They mostly nail
the ones with racing stripes and mag
wheels, not the little Subaru wagons,
Frank says, spraying mousse in his palm,
lifting my hair to an elegant panic.
We are squared off in the mirror.
What's more, the law says they can still
hang you, here, he goes on, for stealing
a horse. I won't, I say. I won't.

KITTY HAWK

Man is not a bird, Wilbur observed.
The trick is to give up flapping

and rolling your own body
between the wings. You must

lie still like a cripple
and trust the gears to warp

and rudder the air
for you. You must work the levers,

give over to your intellect,
rise to objectivity, let the roar

of the motor carry you
up like a surf in your ears.

There you are, going against
everything you believe in—

the Church of the United
Brethren, a whole testament

of necks falling limp
as Sunday chickens, crazed skulls,

your relentless mother,
waving her polkadot handkerchief.

You let the great winged
wheelchair grind you across

the sky. To someone standing
off, *hosannah!* you are a white bird,

a shudder, running out of ground
the way the dead shall rise.

DUNES

We approached the dunes like geometry problems, turning
our bare feet at various angles up

the sand, up to the end of climbing, where things
want to take off. Huge red, yellow, and blue

kites swelled their nylon bellows; hang gliders
slid one-by-one off the edge. We watched

how lifting off speeds up and corrects the line
of ascent or descent, and holds it. Between gravity

and wind, kites stood speechless, ecstatic, invisibly
tethered; gliders caught one moment.

That night I dreamed I had breasts like sand dunes.
They were swollen for a child I barely remembered, but

they leaked milk, so I knew she was mine. I held
her, slick with milk. At the top of the highest dune,

we were conductors: the ocean, the dunes, the holding,
the longing of the child. Energy seethed through us,

making shapes, making what the wind would look like
if it hardened as it rolled out of the mouth of the sky.

ROANOKE: THE LOST COLONY

1

John White, Governor

I took my daughter Elenor, just weeks
from giving birth, and her husband Ananias,
since she begged to go: her vision, mine,
to split the world one cannot help
but split, when time has come to that.
Our small ship put down England there as if
those hundred souls could bring the New
World into consciousness. By Spring, I said,
I'd be returning with supplies. But the wars,
the orders from the Queen—three years
passed like one quick breath, before
the *Hopewell* got me to the spot I'd left
them in. I saw their tree, CROATOAN carved.
No cross, no signal for distress, just
the name of a nearby tribe—like the word
heaven to describe the longing of our short-
term lives for more. Then we had to turn
our crippled boards around and head for home.

I had no cash to try again. I think
my granddaughter must stroke the pelt of some
great bear, listening to her mother tell
of bridges and art, a jumble of a fairy tale.
I see Elenor, year by year opening
the learned rooms of her heart to the loose
branches of the ground, to the stillness
of the fields. I imagine her saying the alphabet

to the child as if its combinations could be
stones to walk on. She will think I'm dead.
She'll say, "No one but God will come
to help us, now, and even He begins to brown
His skin under the sun, and stripe His face
with paint mixed from all the faces
of the earth." This is how I think it is.
I have to let her go, in my mind, go back
into the seasons that kick and fall like
young horses, think of her riding them down
to a steady gait, her taking their reins,
letting them pull the plow deep for her.

2

Elenor Dare, Colonist

I heard my child between my legs cry out,
the first wild naming of my fears. We were
astounded by each other, then. She took
my breast and didn't want to understand, kept
her wants and miseries whole within herself.
It's the same, either shore, what's evil here
or there—dark eyes out of dark trees,
the quick blade through the skin, unmerciful skies—
is what comes over us, what we can't take in
and live. Here we planted our small claim,
corn and beans, potato roots, the smoking-
plant tobacco, not so much with confidence
and grace, as pestered by the rage for living

on, ourselves the seeds cast off by thoughts
not my husband's, father's, or the Queen's.
I'm hardening, calculating, looking in
the eye of love to find it shot clear through
to sky or sea, in language so ordinary,
the in-and-out of breath's enough. England
is a home I'm finished with. Our young men
marry squaws, my own child sits cross-legged
on the longhouse floor and pounds the corn
to bread. Come down, old God and angels to this
place, and watch me eat you up. I put you
in my arms and legs. Every day I'm born again.

BOMBAY HOOK

Out of a great breathing emerge
winged things, a leafing, a shaping, a gathering.
Purple grackle crouch thick as leaves
in the trees. Then at some faint twinge

in the fabric of the day, they are wings,
a black rage in the sky. They are all
like that: starlings like schools of fish,
darting and swarming; thousands of snow-geese

lifting and dropping to the ponds in waves;
even the lone marsh-hawk, glinting
like a huge butterfly, buckles to wind
inside a faultless curve. Before dark,

low tide gathers plovers and pipers
dipping into the muck. The sunset sky
turns restless and winged: so many nights
in the world, who could count them?

The one breath keeps on like a sleeping child
under a down quilt, turning by the will
of a dream, or the twitch of a muscle that knows
what it sends away, and what it holds.

III

AN INTRODUCTION

A little point of contact,
catch of an eye, and I
start fleshing out the whole

beast. He pulls off his
boxer shorts, and we are white
against the linen, afternoon

sun stripping between
blinds. We are ravenous—
only a few moments before,

detailed and courteous. We
have bought a house of bare
wood, rugs in patterns.

Saturday mornings, we look
for chipmunks in the woods
behind our house. We

progress in the ridge
and roll of days, undressing
each other in the dark

openings, almost finding
light enough. It is a short
life until death, his,

at which a number
of angels break out of
his skin and disperse

on urgent assignments,
leaving me with my hands
full of veins, avenues

of deepest faith opening
inside, little points
of contact, drops

of blue ink, diffusing. I
turn all the same color,
heaven come down to earth.

WEATHER

March 12 and 89 degrees—forsythia, tulips, cherry trees
coming out a full month before their time, and all of us

a little crazy from the Global Warming Trend, the hole
in the ozone, or God's Wrath sleepily coming down on us.

I am getting a suntan, having come out here knowing something
will happen, but later, the way the causes of cancer

build up quietly in the cells, the way untranslatable
landscapes wait to be entered, and what can we expect, but

unusual days, anyway, since the divorce rate rose to
fifty percent, and the children started going away, backpacks

full of storybooks for the weekend? The Episcopal Church
is changing its language for God. Who can blame us

for wanting what we can have, taking the heat
as soon as it's available? It's summer in Aruba, anyway,

and who's to say who's right? The weather hasn't done this
for one hundred seventeen years, since records started

to be kept. Before then, maybe, before we got so careful
with the facts, before history, before the rainforests fell.

Are we to blame for the dinosaur's death? the shifting
of the continental plates? Have you ever seen a continental

plate? Don't reason about evil, Dante said, but give
a glance and pass beyond! It is Avidhya, ignorance, to be

transcended and forgotten. But home is so sad, this body
that needs to be lived in and keeps calling us, while

we close the door behind us in one, clear, elemental
move, thinking, *now* our parents will surely give up on us!

BALLROOM DANCING

My father did her hair that night
as he always did, as long
as he talked her into keeping it long.
He'd stand behind her with the hairbrush
and pull her ponytail through
the wire chignon form and tuck and pin
loose ends until it came out tight
and sexy as a seal, just the way
she hated it, and hated his fingertips
cupped around the bun
as if it were a nice fat breast.
He'd ask me to judge
if it was set too low, or high.

That night she was the best I remember
of her, in her three strands of fake
pearls, her glazed white dress
with bird's-wing sleeves and collar.
We walked the two blocks to Mrs. Keller's
dance studio, where we took turns,
parents, then young ladies
and gentlemen, traveling through our box-
steps under lowered lights, then only
fathers with daughters, across
the unsteady surface, my carefully pinned
mother at the side, holding
the ballet bar, both parents lost
to each other. The steps came hard
to me. I brought all my delicate
instrumentation to bear on keeping
my mother's place in the dance
under Mrs. Keller's hard brown eyes.

FOR MICHELLE

We will be old ladies together
on the Outer Banks, our wind chimes going
all day, white curtains blowing
like Daisy's in *The Great Gatsby*,
and they will call us the Brown Sisters,
not separately, and we will ride bikes
four blocks to the library.
You will cook and I will tend the garden.
We will can tomatoes in the fall,
and they will sit in splashy red jars
in the pantry. We will sleep on beds
high enough to need stools. I will sit
on the porch swing and write poems,
brushing our five cats off the page.
Definitely one white, one yellow.
The rest won't matter. We will rock
gently on the swing in the evenings,
and people will wave and stop by.
We will be beloved landmarks.
Neither of us will die during that time.
Days will go along by themselves
and lead nowhere. It will be what
we deserve, what we honed ourselves
to. We will connect what we remember
of our mother, and improve on her.
We will be inside her, arms and legs
of the same happiness. When one of us
thinks tea, the other will get the cups.

FOUR POEMS FOR KELLY

1

When I was your age, you were two years raised
from ether, getting louder. I didn't know
anything: I zipped up your pink cocoon,
clamped down the fat triangular sails
of your diaper. Sometimes the sun crossed
your crib and all the white and folded things,
and I thought I must be loose among
objects. Did you feel the weightless arms
I picked you up with? To this day, you may be
walking your dog, looking in lighted windows
for something you could be held in and know it's you.
You and the dog, holding each other up.
I keep trying to be a house, large-boned. You could
stop by. I would be giving birth to you.

2

We used to drive those dark, pot-bellied house-
shaped cars. Your father and Jack Rose came by
in Jack's Ford—imagine it closing down
on me like a clam, one wet kiss
and slam. This was not sex, but sorrow, fall-
ing inward. It rose up later in your eyes,
that, and a great hard rage of joy. I can
explain neither. There we were, then, trying
not to go too far, making promises
and prayers. It took a long, long time to hear
the answer, and by then you stood skinny

with despair, your heart spread open like a
clam at high tide, watching me turn loose
your house, your father, your only town.

3

What could I save you from, your first summer
at the beach? Poop the drug addict? Zack
the Pittsburgh boxer? The dirty little
room you could afford? I was wrecked
in you. I fixed your Kandy Kitchen bib
and sent you back to work, too sweet, too steeped
in beer. If you had turned from me that summer
I could not have changed it, nor could I now.
The wash of life through us transforms us, or
we sink. We sink anyway. There is my life,
and back of it, the other, writing the poem
the same way you came up from my depths, my dark
shadow and my light, shifting the center
of gravity, pushing death ahead.

4

You say the parents of your friends are break-
ing down: one drinks, one's having an affair,
one cures her husband's headaches by laying on
of hands. We lie side by side in the hammock,
women who've known each other a hundred years,
except for our separate griefs hugged in as if

one word would break the bounds and fuse us back
together. There's that gap. It is Good Friday,
Christ in his tomb, the trees all blossom, breaking
loose again. Nothing but contradictions.
You're going to Philadelphia, sure the world
is made of bricks you walk on, bricks you build
with. Not a word. I'll learn to love
what stands for what. I'll lay hands on your head.

OLGA KNIPPER TO ANTON CHEKHOV, JANUARY 1902

"Gorky's play keeps drawing crowds
(though not to rival yours)
and I play the prostitute Nastya
to such acclaim, I think I have gained
a wanton sway or arch of my neck
from your six weeks with me, here.
Now I have no one to kiss
after the theatre, and no one to feed
his codliver oil. I feel suddenly
ashamed to call myself your wife:
you, in Yalta, depressed and suffering;
I, transforming myself into someone else
each time the curtain lifts.
What sort of wife am I to you?
Write one word, Anton, to bring me there!
Sometimes I think you'd keep me glittering
here, your star in Moscow, living
the life you're now too ill to live.
I'd like to crawl inside your head
until I find the words you'd give
your suffering, and bring them out.
We could say them together,
like two people truly intimate. . . .
If only the baby had lived to be born!
She would have hooked you
to the objects of this world.
You would have cried to me, 'Come see
to this dreadfully broken clown,
or soldier-doll.' Its importance
would have stood between our past
and future like a communion,

a collision of laughing and weeping.
There would have been no more of this
level indifference, this long look
over the top of the day's events
toward night, and more night."

SNOW

My steps leave nothing alone, press and
press, to make the snow groan beneath
my feet. The trains still come, up on
the hill, clouding the rails with snow
like the fast retreat of horses, or
romance. Down here, my old self keeps on
going. So many kinds of love have passed
through me like the blue overhead spark
of trains, the way it flies along
the wires and leaves them still. Each
time I have come back to myself prickly
and muffled among the essential forms
of snow. I used to follow my father's
feet: I have been lonely since, and maybe
I was lonely then. A flag of some buried
gift has remained like a twig, the lost
whistle of it struck up. I keep
making these tracks as if they mattered,
as if circling and digging, I
could scent out the portal home. Always,
the snow has stung like a longing.

THEN YOU FALL IN LOVE, AT YOUR AGE

All afternoon, your fingers climb
the little hills of his hands.
The thought you climb out of is deep
as death, and renews itself minute
by minute, a well filling with water
you have been drinking from for years
until you thought you weren't thirsty.
Look how it turns the color
of sky and evergreens, turns inward
like a reflection!
All the times you've failed to love
well, or that you've turned away,
are lifted on its surface like clouds.
Nothing in the world cares
whether you hold his hand. Necessity sits
serene as a saint, looking up
or down, and in between, you find
yourself (yes!) willing. About all
there has ever been is hands,
after you moved out of the cities
of your houses and books.
How early can you remember love, its
old cloth textures, the lifting
in the air against all odds, and enough
flesh at last against your cheek
to open you past yourself? It's as much
the last time as the first,
as permanent as your knuckles
and wrists, the way they grew without
you, into somebody else, still you.

SUN GOING DOWN

We stayed to watch the sun go down.
Odd rocks, eroded in folds and curls
sucked the waves under.

It was a long dazzle, clouds
lit from inside, then under, then
the quick dance and slide of light

into a pocket of hills. At our feet
a bowling ball washed up like a dark sun!
I lifted it out, bowled through

sand into driftwood, not
making a strike, but remembering
in my body the stance, the turn

of wrist. "Can you really bowl?"
he asked me, and luck ran
all through my arms and legs,

the luck of bumping the cracked
ball toward any wild twist of wood,
the luck of keeping no score.

There I was, lighting a Tareyton
with my Razorback Zippo. Fayetteville,
the old Benton Lanes

on Dickson Street, twelve thunderclap
alleys, my old acrid life,
how hard I had tried. Then I was

Rip Van Winkle, come home to
a strange and softer town. The sun
struck the loosestrife, and went down.

BREAD

I dump the whole-wheat flour into the pale
and breathless yeast, wet and waking to
itself, slight whispers of yeast, now, exhaled
between the kneading of my hands. I loop
the dough. It tenses and fights back. It is
an ear—turned and turned into an ear—
listening deep into its own new fist
of energy, where the long austere
sleep of the wheat is broken. It and I
are separate, contending fists, listening
to the space between us, our borders surprised
by our opposite work. We come up with a system:
three times we do not know each other. We swell
ourselves up. Our reunion is tender, heart-felt.

ELVIS AT THE END OF HISTORY

It was him, Elvis, sheepishly
stepping out of my outhouse,
looking better than ever, the way
some old men slim down and loosen
their lines. He had left the door open,
the lid slightly ajar on the women's
hole. As usual, I forgave him
everything. I acted normal, as if
I hadn't been waiting under the trees,
last night's full chamber-pot
balanced in my hand. I could have
said at any point in my life
that he was the one I was waiting for,
looking sleepily down from the stage,
seeing but not seeing me,
granting me reprieve in an instant
from my life, but holding me in it
like a star. It's like if you ask
for Jesus, Jesus comes. It's never
the way you think. There he was,
hair flopped over his eyes,
coming out of the last outhouse left
along the lake, and it there
only because of the grandfather clause.
This was the end of our history
together, all that strangeness
in the crotch, the pulse hammering
the bass line, real life and art
straining to fuse, to end all
history. I was hearing in my mind

Won't you wear my ring,
around your neck? but it sounded
like the sweet core of good taste,
like the gospel fleshed out,
saddened down to honky tonk.
"Excuse me," he said. "The older I get,
the more often I have to pee."
I agreed. I might have been humming
to myself, sometimes I don't know
when I'm doing it. I can be
treble and bass at the same time.

IV

PROPELLER-BIKE

1

It still feels like I'm
riding, past the airport, past
fields, knowing what's left
behind in town: the little
breakfast on Melmac, juice
in colored aluminum
tumblers, my brother Mark
in his pajamas, strapped
in his custom-built
adult-size highchair, slinging
a spoonful of oatmeal
at the wall as he blanks
and grips into a seizure, all
his muscles pulling
inward as if there were
a nub of comfort at the core.
A catch, and a waking
into his groan, the animal-
cry that still breaks
out of my dreams, waking
my husband.

2

Before breakfast in Columbia,
Missouri, in 1951, morning
zipped along the spiderwebs,
the College Club Dairy truck

rattled the driveway, and I
put on striped T-shirt
and shorts. Already, my father
was under the walnut tree,
carving and sanding,
worrying over the pitch
and slip of the propeller.
He explained gravity
and centrifugal force
to me, those invisible
requirements one tricks,
one uses, to escape.
I squatted close to the
evidence, tried to learn,
not wanting to be left behind.

3

We invent our heroes
to let us approach the truth.
We imagine they're the ones
who worry, instead of us:
my father, worrying over his
Schwinn, trying to get it
to screw the air
like a hummingbird with a used
single-cylinder Briggs
and Stratton motor. It is
my father, barely
holding vector rotation

to the pavement, tracing his
greasy fingers like a blind man
toward the absolute edge
of the law.

City police told him, ask
the city attorney. City attorney
assured him no such device
would be permitted
in town. Sergeant Ben Booth
of the Missouri State
Highway Patrol, who was later
heroically shot in the line
of duty, said the city
would have to let him use it, if
he got a motorcycle license.

4

Down 40, past the airport
runway, past corn and soybeans,
it roared like a plane, tore up
a coupling. My father adjusted,
balanced, carved a new
propeller, different
pitch, set up a system of
pulleys and belts. Next door,
my grandparents watched
out the window, knowing he
could never do anything right.

Afternoons, my grandmother scoured
the sprouts of dark hair
off my legs with Baby-Touch.
         "Sandpapering your legs,"
my father called it. Also,
she locked my fingers into
the microscopic laws of piano
lessons. The top of my head
was all propeller, almost as if
I invented the day we
loaded clothes and toys
into an open trailer, tarp
desperately fluttering away
from the center, toward Arkansas,
where my father at last got
his bike to go twenty-
seven-and-a-half miles per
hour, timed for a mile
with no wind, cheap as dirt
to run, where he took me
for a ride, holding me
in his lap, where my mother
sat on a blanket in the backyard,
drying her hair in the sun,
where Mark crashed
and crashed his handsome face
into permanent grotesqueries
which looked just like him
after all.

5

But my father had to stop
for every dog, to keep
the blade from lopping off
its head. He soldered
aluminum wire into a
propeller-guard, which
ruined the efficiency,
caused the front wheel
to shimmy. The bike fell
backwards from the weight.
And in wet weather, dirt
and rocks nibbled
at the blade until he
had to carve it down.
He began to doubt
the practicality. I kissed
a boy, whirled out
in circle skirts, petti-
coats crackling, stayed out
past midnight, took off
my clothes one by one
growing lighter and faster
against the old animal
catch and groan
planted on a side
road like a police car.

My mother at the children's pool with Mark. The other
women are holding their own, delicately splashing their

perfect sons, trying to stay between one thought
and the next. All our lives, keeping our eyes front,

our bodies turned at appropriate angles
toward the audience. I demonstrate handing the normal

plastic rings back to my brother, pulling him
around the rim: engine, caboose. My mother in white shorts

stirs the water with her feet, an action which
enrages me, her small feet a condition of the body.

If I fall into my body now, I will drown. Mark is
taking off through water on tiptoe, the tendons in his

ankles drawn permanently tight. A woman
next to my mother has asked her, "What's wrong with him?"

In the big pool, I stand on the scaffold
of the high dive, appealing. Once my own son fell against

the edge of the children's pool, a little red smile
under his chin, spreading. It's not as if one event stands

beside another, separated by a delicate
membrane. It's all done through images, the blood of fear,

of rage, soaking through the towel. The woman in the red
hybiscus-splattered mumu beside my mother makes her

daughter hand Mark back the ring. The daughter inches
forward, watching her own feet, aware of her audience.